O Beautiful Dust

O Beautiful Dust

Walking the Wilderness Toward Common Prayer

RW Walker

Squirrel House Publishing

O Beautiful Dust:
Walking the Wilderness Toward Common Prayer
ISBN: 9781951882198
Copyright © 2014, 2022 Robert Walker

All rights reserved. No portion of this book may be reproduced or transmitted in any form or by any means without permission from the publisher, except as permitted by U.S. copyright law, fair use, and in the case of brief quotations embodied in critical articles and reviews. For permissions, please reach out to the publisher at questions@squirrelhousepub.com
Cover & formatting by SJ Blasko

Squirrel House Publishing
squirrelhousepub.com
instagram.com/squirrelhousepub

"This Lent poetry collection is a much needed resource for queer Christians today. Instead of proclaiming the message of judgement and "you'll always fall short" that I often find in evangelical books, this raw and honest collection of poetry spills over with the message of hope that we are deeply loved, each one of us is created in God's image, and it challenges us to go forth into the world as our most authentic selves that God created us to be."

—Sara Baysinger, author of *The Vanishing Spark of Dusk*

"We have a job to do that we are not doing."
"With this challenge, Rob Walker dares to hope that our Lenten meditations can empower us to build Christian bridges over chasms that now threaten our civic and spiritual lives. If issuing this call were his only aim, it would be enough. But Beautiful Dust is so much more. Walker's evocative poems invite us to see, really to see, the grit and glitter on Jesus's 40-day hike to Jerusalem. This slender volume will accompany me on my own Lenten journey this year, and what fine company it is."

-- Rev. Elizabeth M. Edman, author of *Queer Virtue: What LGBTQ People Know About Life and Love and How It Can Revitalize Christianity*

"O Beautiful Dust serves as a thoughtful prayer companion for traversing the complexities of the liturgical season of Lent. With prayers that are lyrical, profound, and occasionally playful, Walker applies deeply personal emotions to communal concerns, inspiring contemporary pilgrims to navigate the multi-faceted mysteries of Divine Love while confronting the uncomfortable challenges of neighborly love. Like the psalms of old, O Beautiful Dust creates a space to pray, praise, and lament through difficult subjects such as politics and peace, identity, doubt, and grief in a manner that encourages intimacy with God and openness to the people God created. I am confident this book will make an uplifting addition to the Lenten devotional practices of its readers."

—Chloe S. Flanagan, pastor and inspirational fiction author

"Walker's collection, *Oh Beautiful Dust,* is a heartfelt exploration of hard questions, deep hungers, and dark places--where a call to love and a prayer for hope become a voice of peace for a grieving, weighted generation."

—Mariella Taylor, *The Folded World*

For James Alec Dixon, the love of my life:
You add so much joy—and stir.
I wouldn't have it any other way.

For Duncan Broom,
who waited so patiently for the first edition,
his birthday gift:
You have been a steady and joy-full presence on the Way.
O man: You are not forgotten. Play your song often.[1]

For Brother Ignatius Feaver, who walked with me for a
season as a spiritual director:
You always invited me to love the Lord passionately,
alongside my truest self.

And (not least) for God's Rainbow People, moving to meet
around God's throne.

"You are the Beloved."

---

[1] Adapted from a song by Jenny Moore, st. benedict's table, Winnipeg, MB.

Table of Contents

Preface (2013) Praying in the Wilderness	iii
Preface (2022) Common Prayer in the Wilderness? An Update	viii
A note on inclusive language and the use of Scripture	xv
Preparation	1
Lent One	11
Lent Two	19
Lent Three	33
Lent Four	45
Lent Five	59
Passion Week	75
After the Easter Vigil	92
The Sunday of the Resurrection of Jesus Christ	94

Preface (2013)
Praying in the Wilderness

[Author's Note, 2022: I enclose minor amendments to this preface in square brackets.]

How this book came together
"What are you giving up for Lent?"

This question often provokes a wry grin in many Christian churches as Lent approaches. Lent is a time of preparation for Easter—a time of learning about the Christian faith, and of amendment of life. To aid Christians in this preparation, the churches usually recommend three spiritual practices: fasting, prayer, and almsgiving, or assistance to the poor. By focusing on "giving up something," I wonder if some people (including me, I think) silently think God delights in temporarily suspending the fun in our lives!

But I find the image of "making room for the spaciousness of God" much more evocative and helpful. If what we desire in Lent is a deeper relationship with

God and the strength to be our truest selves, then the traditional practices make a lot more sense: we fast to make space for new encounters with God (in prayer) and new generosity toward our neighbours (by giving alms).

Like many people nowadays, I spend a lot of time on Facebook. I asked my friends there what they thought about me "giving up" Facebook for Lent. The general consensus went something like this: "Only if it helps your relationship with God and with others." A surprising number said: "But your Facebook posts are so helpful—they are part of your ministry; please don't give them up."

Many of my Facebook posts are short prayers, usually in a style called a "collect," in which I try to express what many people might be feeling and thinking on a given day or about a given topic or situation. In the last year, several very wise friends have said to me unbidden, "You should write a book." [I wrote the first edition of this book for Duncan Broom and Br. Ignatius Feaver, two men who taught me my belovedness-in-God.] I did decide to reduce greatly my

Facebook presence—but I added the practice of trying deliberately to express an important thought or prayer at least once a day.

My practice wasn't perfect, as any reader who is a stickler for dates will find out [in the pages of the first edition]! I also found that it was strange to have part of my prayer life so deliberately "out in public": there is a danger in wanting "only to be seen by people" as it says in the Gospel of Matthew. Nevertheless, I found that it felt a lot like doing what Anglicans usually call the "Prayers of the People"—the praying became not just about me, but about how God could fit all of us into God's plans.

The Structure and Goals of this Book
Ash Wednesday is always the start of Lent, preceded by a day of preparation often called Shrove Tuesday or Mardi Gras. The Sundays until Palm Sunday (the beginning of Holy or Passion Week) are numbered consecutively. Though it is not required to read the book in anything like linear order, reading them this way might allow you to share with me what my own spiritual journey was like as I "walked the wilderness"

liturgically with Jesus. The book ends with two prayers on the Feast of the Resurrection of Jesus: Easter Sunday. God was teaching me about love, expressed as gratitude, and fear, that spiritual force that often seems to block our experience of God's profound goodness in our lives.

I am a gay Christian with traditional theology [by which I mean: I want to be a Nicene Christian who affirms and celebrates the faithful relationships and gifts of Two Spirit, lesbian, gay, bisexual, trans, intersex, & asexual/aromantic people in Christian communities]. I find Christian teaching about the Trinity to be deeply beautiful and meaningful. The stories of Scripture, to me and to most Christians, are an amazing resource from which to learn about God and what God is "up to" with human and universal history. [Maintaining this kind of perspective in today's world proves difficult for many followers of Messiah Jesus, including me.] We live in a world that finds thinking in terms of stories and symbols very difficult, because we don't really believe that stories and symbols are true: "Just the facts, ma'am."

I offer these prayers hoping that they can be a basically adequate vehicle for God to reveal His reality and how She operates in the world. Some scholars I appreciate call this revelation through symbol and story "Christian symbolic imagination." Facts are crucial to our faith—Jesus Christ was born, lived, was executed [by the Roman Empire], and rose again from the dead—but these facts must lead us further on, to a new picture of how God-as-Jesus runs the world—which looks so opposite to our usual dog-eat-dog, there's-never-enough-to-go-around notions!

Blessings and peace [to you and yours]! May these prayers help us all to imagine and to appreciate the beauty of Jesus Christ even more deeply. God helping us, let us show forth that beauty in our own lives, every day.

Rob Daywalker
Easter Week, 2013

Preface (2022)
Common Prayer in the Wilderness? An Update

The first edition of this book feels like it was written half-a-lifetime ago. I was beginning PhD studies by distance learning in the UK; these prayers were written before an ankle injury permanently changed how I experience my mobility; and (not least) I had no idea I was living with clinical anxiety and ADHD whilst somewhere on the autism spectrum—I just called it "CP brain" then. I remember 2013 being a year full of conflict. And yet I lived a good life—and I still do.

Fast forward to February 2022, and things have shifted decisively—not just for me, but for the entire planet! Think of it: Barack Obama finished two terms in the White House, battling unspoken but obvious racism the whole way; Donald "You're Fired!" Trump not only ran for, but occupied the office of, the President of the United States; partisan violence and fear-mongering is breaking out; nobody in their right mind can ignore the climate change emergency anymore; and as I write this, the COVID-19 pandemic continues into its third year, exposing the deep economic inequities and systemic racism of "business as usual" (especially in Canada and the US) in unprecedented ways.

What bothers me the most
Of all these complicated and mostly awful things, one bothers me above all. For the last decade especially, people have forgotten how to disagree respectfully—in fact, I'd go so far as to say that a sizable portion of those who live in the countries called the US and Canada have forgotten what it means to have meaningful conversations. As a good friend of mine put it recently, "When I can't disagree with someone in good faith without becoming their enemy, it's terrifying." And yet that's where the culture is, by-and-large. Cultural commentators and social scientists of all political and methodological persuasions have been weighing in, and I think most of their contributions have tremendous value.

A call to love across deep difference
But since this is a book of prayers for Lent—a season for deliberately re-aligning our lives with the Commonwealth of God known through the ministry of

Jesus—let me speak to my fellow Christians, my fellow poets, and all people in the US and Canada who long to pray & love well:

We have a job to do that we are currently *not* doing.

By-and-large, Christians (including me!) are failing to lean into what the New Testament calls "the ministry of reconciliation." When we have researchers telling us that a growing number (perhaps a large majority) of people in North America believe that "people 'on the other side' can destroy the world," let me ask all-y'all a question:

How are people going to resist this lie if Spirit-empowered, Love-fired people don't model deep love (including loving debate) across strong disagreement?

I am aware that there's an irony, here: a white, Nicene Creed-affirming, disabled, queer Christian who is firmly on the political and social left is calling for dialogue and love? Some people might hear me as discounting harm; others might hear me as valuing sentimentality over truth-telling. I hope I'm doing neither. After all, loving

God, my neighbour, and myself—truthfully, fully, compassionately—is a lifetime's seriously playful work!

I have a burning desire to see increasing numbers of people(s) decide to confront potential disagreement with all of Love's available resources. I want (especially) those of us who are largely healed from life's major injuries—and (particularly) those who have advantages because they are in the majority—to intervene, simply and radically (i.e., "going to the root"). For example:

- Take folks we disagree with out for long coffee dates to talk about things that matter.
- Start blogs, magazines, and publishing houses.
- Learn Nonviolent Communication and other skillsets.
- Deliberately break the easy echo chambers of our social media.
- Boost the voices of people who are most affected by social problems but have the least access to resources.
- Incorporate practices into our lives that expand empathy and sharpen critical thinking skills.
- Join peacemaking organizations.

- Learn Mental Health First Aid and other crisis intervention strategies.
- Be more suspicious-but-loving of ourselves and our cloudy, jagged motivations.

All these things show, in their different ways, deep respect and love across difference.

I believe it is crucial for the flourishing of our society and its people(s) to "say" with our lives something like the following:

> I am here in good faith, and I love you. 'Agreeing to disagree' isn't gonna cut it anymore—it stokes too much fear and causes too much harm. Let's talk through [name of issue/problem] until we understand each other. What is the extent of our agreement? How can I show love and respect to you and yours even while we disagree? What can we do together to strengthen our society, our communities, ourselves?

One possible antidote: Common Prayer
Many of the prayers in the first edition felt to me like being someone responsible for the Prayers of the People

(a time of communal prayer during a worship service). Even in situations where using "I" felt appropriate, I was trying to pray in ways that would resonate with the concerns of many. Paradoxically, specific detail often helps. But I believe that where the resonance happens, where large numbers of people are able and willing to say, "Amen" (literally, "I agree"), we find a kind of community—I'd even dare to call it a politics—that cuts across and starts to dissolve buzzwords and jargon and hardened political stances.

I am hoping and praying, I think, for what my Anglican friends call "common prayer"—and I hope these prayers can contribute in some small way. I know that the Spirit's call to me—and (I think) also to the larger crowd of Spirit-people for the foreseeable future—is to help enlarge my/our capacity for loving conversation and loving disagreement.

I am so grateful to S.J. Blasko, and the good people of Squirrel House Press, for the opportunity to revise and reissue this book—I am confident that their future work will move people toward more loving conversation! Many of the prayers in this revised edition reflect the daily Bible readings for Year C in the Revised Common Lectionary (a three-year cycle of Bible readings used in many mainline Christian churches), though my focus is on the theme of "Walking the Wilderness Toward Common Prayer."

Even if our convictions are vastly different, Dear Reader, I invite you to walk the wilderness with me in common prayer, reflection, and (often difficult) hope. Perhaps we'll find out, together, how to embrace the agenda of the Kingdom of God—Christ's own—just a little more.

Even so, come quickly, Lord Jesus!

RW Walker
Feast of St. Valentine, 2022

A note on inclusive language and the use of Scripture

I believe in inclusive language. For me, the best term for it is "expansive language," where all the images and names that are so important to Christian tradition are still "in play," alongside more 'experimental' language which is consistent with the character of the God known in, through, and as Jesus the Christ. Each generation of Christians needs to articulate their trust in God in terms that resonate in their contexts.

For myself, I have done a lot of work to heal God-images of Father and Lord, so I include them here. It is my conviction that I cannot heal any problems I have with God (or my picture of God) if I deliberately avoid *forever* the things which have wounded me. Your mileage may vary, and that's totally OK. If you find these prayers valuable, please feel free to adapt them to your context.

As a post-Evangelical (and still Pentecostal) Anglican Christian, sometimes engaging with Scripture "devotionally" still causes me trouble, though it is my heart's desire to appropriate and read the Scriptural narratives as Jesus would. Where it seems appropriate, I have suggested a reading which either inspired the composition of a particular prayer or includes its themes. If engaging Scripture "devotionally" is helpful to you, feel free to make use of these suggestions.

Preparation

Streamline Our Hearts, Jesus
Shrove Tuesday/Mardi Gras

Streamline our hearts, Jesus:

We are about to walk with you into the wilderness.

May our leanness in coming days
mean that we give away your riches.

May the riches of your presence
make us willing to join your revolution.
May the lives we live
be a bright and warm invitation
into your Kingdom.

Cause us to preserve all the good we encounter in your world by dying:
to selfish ego,
to privilege,
to despair.

Show the world, through us,
a glimpse of your Resurrection,

and the fiery love of your Holy Spirit.

Help us to make room for you.
Amen.

O Beautiful Dust
Ash Wednesday

Lord, I remember that I am dust,
and that I will return to it:
But O, what beautiful dust!

You have regarded me in my smallness,
making me your representation and shadow:
And O, what beautiful dust!

Therefore, I sing to you,
Word made flesh who lived, and died, and rose—

Glory to You, O Beautiful Dust!
Amen.

Losing My Own Soul? (Luke 9:8-25)
Thursday

Jesus,

I want to agree with Peter:
"You are God's Messiah."

I am willing to die for you, Lord!
It even sounds exciting:
Only revolutionaries get crucified.
(Much better than obsessing over my own personal sins, no?)

But at the risk of sounding whiny:
What "cross" is mine, exactly?

I'm already in a "world" that crucifies me
as I love men while living with CP.
It says (under its breath):
You have no soul to lose!

I trust you, Jesus, to keep my soul.
If I can't have you,

I wouldn't want the world anyway.

Amen.

As Though It Were Nothing (Jeremiah 32:27)
Friday

Holy Spirit, beloved friend:

I don't know why you use one prayer
to change my life.

But as a friend prayed for me
about Fear surrounding
my writing and public speaking,
he asked you to "wash it away
as though it were nothing."

And you did
—a cool shiver running down my back.
Is anything too hard for you?

In these days of Fear
(Whether of disease, political combat,
or economic and social dysfunction)
we cry:
"Wash it away as though it were nothing!"

And do it, please, through us.
Amen.

"The Fear" (Genesis 31:42)
Saturday

Sovereign and gracious Lord:

Your friend Isaac called you "the Fear."
What kind of relationship did he have with you?
Did he (always) believe
that you were going to take him from himself?

Did he learn to rest in you,
knowing that you kept him alive,
even though his father was a fundamentalist?

Did he—like me, like most of us—
wonder and wander between these poles,
sometimes camping near one,
sometimes the other?

Sustain us with your life and steadfast love.

Teach us never to scorn those
for whom you are "the Fear,"
but lead us gently

on Love's more excellent Way.

Amen.

Lent One

Allow us, O God... (Luke 4:1-13)
Sunday

Allow us, O God, to experience your spaciousness:
Not by inventing a procedure,
but by seeking your heart...

Allow us, O God, to experience your power:
Not by evading hard questions,
but by trusting your kindness...

Allow us, O God, to experience your love:
Not by putting you to the test,
but by accepting that you accept our questions...

Allow us, O God, to walk through this Lent:
Not by evading our deep hungers and dark places,
but by trusting that your voice
is our truest bread and water…

…even in Jesus Christ, your Son, our Lord.
Amen.

The Place of Open-Heartedness (Romans 2:3-4)
Monday

Lord, your kindness leads us to repentance —

to change of mind and heart,
to turning around,
to a new agenda and direction.

Lead us to the place where our friends and enemies
—our neighbours both and all—
will experience the kindness that leads
to transformation:
ours and theirs.

We ask this for Jesus' honour:
Amen.

"SHUT UP!" *(Mark 4:35-41)*
Tuesday

Lord of storms:

Some days feel like a sudden mighty spasm of the sea,
when all we wanted was to row our boat.

Then, suddenly, all is at peace,
because we hear you shout at the waves:

"SHUT UP!"

Thank you.

Lord of Healing (John 5:1-14)
Wednesday

Lord Jesus, walking near the Pool:

Thank you that as the waters stir,
healing may not be far behind, whether
in the waters themselves,
in the sound of your voice asking if we want to be well,
in the strength of your grasp
as you set us right without blame or shame—

because you hear "YES!"
when all we know to do is rehearse our grievances.

Lead us to trust you while life churns,
because we know that you have not forgotten us.

Amen.

The Altar at Mamre (Genesis 13:1-18)
Thursday

God of Abraham and Sarah,
Whose plans for us are for good and not for ill:

At the crossroads of life,
In places of indecision,
Engage us in conversation with you.

Direct us to honour those around us,
And to discern your treasures
beneath superficial appearances,
that our lives may be infused with gratitude.

For the honour of your Name:
Amen.

Birth (Romans 8:18-39)
Friday

Holy Spirit,

You search the deep things of the heart,
and work to adjust, heal, transform —

even while, even if, we feel nothing.

Bring to birth and growth
those deep things
you are gestating in us,

even if, groaning with you,
we are the last to see them through tear-filled eyes.

Amen.

A Blessing (Psalm 42)
Saturday

Friends:
Go in peace—and in pieces,
Practicing the Presence of the Living God;
everything else flows from here.
Thanks be to God.

Lent Two

Thanks (Isaiah 49:8-13)
Sunday

Living, gracious God:

Thank you for the gift of life, today.
Thanks for calling all people to be your friends.
Thank you for the wilderness walk of Jesus.
Thanks for calling *me* your friend.

Make your people joyful in this season
of clearing space;
bring us closer to living
the kind of life
which pleases you and
liberates the world.

In Jesus' Name:
Amen.

Obedience
Monday

Dangerous One,

So many of us have heard the call to obedience
as silencing our genuine questions.

A church hierarch,
a parent,
a teacher,
a televangelist says,

"Agree with me—
or suffer the punishment of God!"

Convince us, instead, that obedience arises
from good listening,
from faithful wrestling,
from robust debate and conversation—
and above all, from a deep knowing:
You call us Beloved.

Thank you that—where 'obedience' is concerned—

you give us enough time to learn what it means.

Amen.

On International Women's Day [2] ***(Amos 5:24)***
Tuesday

Jesus, borne by Mary,
I thank you for women —
cis, nonbinary, trans, anywhere from straight to queer,
all the shades of the good earth —
each and all made in your image and
called to bear your likeness.

Allow us to see the women around us
rise to their full dignity, because
until justice rolls down like waters for all women,
none of us are totally — truly — free,
because we rise and fall together.

When the time is right, bring us to the city of light,
where everyone — daughters and sons,
friends and lovers, all peoples together —
shall dwell together in safety.

In the meantime:
We rise,

---

[2] Inspired by Maya Angelou's "Still I Rise".

We rise,
We rise.

Amen.

Of More-than-Enough
Wednesday

Just and gracious sovereign:

Teach us about your Kingdom,
which is not like Egypt,
not like Rome,
not like Western capitalism.

Show us what it means to live in your economy:
of grace-gift, of joy-directed love,
of more-than-enough.

Teach us not to sell each other out,
but to see in each face we meet
a bearer of your living image,
each one called to become your likeness.

We ask this for the honour of Jesus
the One whom humanity sold out,
but who (nevertheless!) is alive and reigning
with you and the Holy Spirit, One God

through countless ages.

Amen.

A Public Secret (Psalm 29)
Thursday

Living, gracious God:
We split you open, trying to silence your voice
when it sang God's justice, healing, and peace;
yet you pour yourself out.

Your love drips and flows into our brokenness,
gathering us up without conditions,
but still with marvelous hopes.

No conditions, truly!
And yet your love, when it touches us, transforms:
Bones made strong, hearts woven new,
silenced tongues breaking into song.

It feels like a public secret:
All of creation wakes up,
remembers what it is for and whose it is,
when you move among your people,
singing: "Glory!"

We agree.

Unconditional Love
Friday

Unconditional Love:
You call us by our true names,
and you see us at our worst.

Enfold us all when we have no energy to try.
Assure us that you deem us "enough."

After all, you love us—your neighbours—
as you love yourself!

We are bold to pray this way
because of Jesus, your Love-made-flesh.

Amen.

For (even) "Those People" [Explicit Language Warning]
Saturday

We bless you, Lord, for "those people":

Who teach us our dignity and worth,
Who coax us into our uniqueness,
Who sing to us of a better world and of our place in it,
Who challenge us to do better.

We bless you, Lord, for "those people":

Who feed and clothe the poor,
Who wonder *why* there are poor and move toward poverty's destruction,
Who are poor—and make us uncomfortable by their presence.

We bless you, Lord, for "those people":

Who are courageous enough to call out our bullshit,
Who take our displaced angers and ask good questions,
Who help us heal by holding up a mirror,

Who hold us when we wonder if we are hopeless
assholes when shame comes a-stalking.

We bless you, Lord, for "those people":
Who still believe things we've outgrown,
Who harm people by their ignorance,
Who deny science, and systemic racism, and human
caused climate change,
Who think the disabled and mentally ill should "get it
together,"
Who think queer people and immigrants are unravelling
the fabric of society.

Yes, Lord, even "those people":

Because you command us to love them as the only way
to be free,
Because we're free only when you help us confront
the shit which rises when we try to pray this way,
Because we are—because I am—part of somebody else's
"those people."

Therefore, I am blessing you for me,

And we are blessing you for us.

Lord, in your kindness: hear our prayer.

Lent Three

Smell Test (Luke 13:1-9)
Sunday

Hey, God,

Show us your character.

Do you draw a straight line:
good behaviour to blessing, bad behaviour to disaster?

Are you the one wanting to chop down the 'slow' tree?
The one who asks for another year?

Because you are not at war with yourself;
because you are Love;
and
because you, the Love that made all things,
chose to become human as Jesus the Messiah:

When we ask questions about your character,
lead us only to answers that smell just like him.

We ask this because of his character, which is only and
always yours:

Amen.

I Am Not the Only One
Monday

Hey, God:

i.
Sometimes my prayers are very public.
Sometimes they seem a little half-baked.

Sometimes it seems they fly up,
only to hit a brass sky, and flop back to the earth.

Sometimes it seems
Like all of Hell rises to stop them,
Choking off the sounds my soul tries to make.

Sometimes I doubt you want to hear me
Because the darkness of shame seems
Like my only friend.

Sometimes I wonder if I pray (especially here)
because I like the sound of my own voice.

ii.
But sometimes, it is good to know
that I am not the only one
singing-shouting-crying at top-of-lungs or barely-in-whispers,
because as much as I love you, there is a much bigger *we*.

You rouse us and cause us to be faithful to you—
Your gentleness makes us great.

"Break us open, Lord," keep it real—
make us pray-ers, and part of your answers to our prayers.

Let all God's friends and lovers say:
Yes, please!

My Delight is in You (Genesis 32)
Tuesday

Holy Spirit,

I used to pray to you, a lot like this:
"I love you. You suck!"
Thank you for understanding.

I remember reading:
"Teacher, do you not care that we are about to die?"
"Will not the Judge of all the earth do right?"
"I will not let you go until you bless me!"

I begin to see that you allowed such prayers,
even encouraged them
because you wanted my friendship.

When I realise this,
I feel very, very small,
and yet: "Your gentleness has made me great."

Help me to delight in your friendship
still more, and may my life give you

the honour you deserve.

In the name of Jesus and for the glory of the Father: Amen.

Writing Might Get Me Killed
Wednesday

Murdered One:

Your nonviolent witness shook everything to its foundations.
You were and are the Language of God in human flesh—
Silenced, but only for a moment.
I must admit feeling curious about the conversations you had with God.
How did you negotiate who you were?
How did you tell the truth—how *were* you Truth—
against every pressure to lie?

I think you call me, too, to negotiate who I am.
Never completely alone, but always in community.

But sometimes, there is so much pressure
to speak and write and *be* a certain way,
and I just can't.

I am not as good as you are at resisting lies.
But if you and I are writing my life together,
if I am your icon, "written,"
a "masterpiece" through which you touch
the world you love so much:

Teach me to write "in some basically adequate way without lying."[3]
Teach me to hold my integrity as a precious and living gift.
Teach me, if and when I lie, to look for your rescue—to begin again.

Telling the truth might get me "killed" in so many different ways—but teach me the joy of the Resurrection.
Cause the "writing" of truth—and Truth—in my life.

Amen.

---

[3] A quote from queer theologian Mark D. Jordan when I met him at Trinity College, Toronto.

Full Maturity (Ephesians 4:1-16)
Thursday

Rabbi,

O how I love sitting—in person—with your friends:
to ask hard questions
to heal my heart,
to hear your words,
to share a meal.

Allow your friends and lovers the grace
to hear your voice when other direction seems lacking,
to remember that love does no harm to the neighbour,
to embrace the joy of growing into your full maturity.

I—and we—want to be like you.

Even so,
Come, Lord Jesus.

Thank You for My Life
Friday

Full and wonderful God:

Thank you for the gifts of my life.

For the people who love and challenge me, even on my worst days: [name them here].

For people to love, and challenge, and love into speech: [name them here].

For mentors, and those who give me guidance: [name them here].

For the graces of my good body, frail though it is: [name them here].

Thank you for my inestimable value in your eyes.

Amen.

A Blessing
Saturday

My dear friends:

God makes us, defends us, and loves us,
Small though we are.

Though the world is in chaos,
Though evil comes in like a flood,
I assure you in the name of Jesus
(through his beloved, Julian of Norwich):
"All shall be well,
and all shall be well,
and all manner of thing shall be well."

Be at rest, beloved people,
because the Most Holy Trinity
Delights in you,
and defends you on every side.

Go now in peace—and in pieces—
Until we meet again.
Amen.

Lent Four

Simple Joys (John 15:9-17)
Sunday

Thank you, gracious God, for the joy of simply being
with friends:
to receive your Word and Sacraments;
to eat together at table;
to find joy in conversation;
to rest at the end of a long day.

Thank you, above all, for your joy in us;
let us find our fullest joy in you.

We ask this in the name of Jesus,
the One who calls us His friends:

Amen.

Something Remarkable (1 Corinthians 1:26-31)
Monday

There is something remarkable, O God,
about how you bless small acts of courage.

There is something bold, O God,
about how you use the weak things to shake the strong.

There is something subversive, O Marvelous God,
about how you make the "useless" things
remarkable, beautiful, enough.

In our courage,
boldness,
weakness,
uselessness,
and beauty,
we ask:

Form in us your image
and gift us the likeness of your Son,

Jesus the Anointed, our Sovereign.

That would be enough.
Amen.

A Heart Like Yours
Tuesday

Thank you, Creator, for artists—
of all kinds, shapes,
sizes and abilities.

Thank you for all who want to tell the truth,
as creative, liberating forces in your good world.

Sometimes art—and truth telling—can look so simple.
Yet there is learning, skill, pain, joy, sweat, tears
—sheer heart—under, in and through all these things.

Sometimes hearts—like mine—feel so
mis-appreciated,
misunderstood,
even misdirected.

Would you grow, in me, a heart
that notices,
appreciates,
understands,
loves—

a heart like yours.

Amen.

Word/s (Luke 3:21-22)
Wednesday

O Gracious Light:

You were able to speak words of life
(and you continue to speak them)
even when misunderstood, ignored, reviled.

You are the Eternal Word, yet we tried (and try)
to still your voice,
to silence your call
to destroy each other's joy and peace.

Forgive us—forgive me—
when the words I speak do not match your character.
I often wound those who are so important to me,
and (how much more!) to you.

Sustain us as we learn to speak love truly,
and whisper over us the Word that will set us right:
"This is my Beloved, in whom I delight."

By the Gift of your own Uncreated Light,

transform the words we say
and how we say them.

Amen.

The Gift of Life
Thursday

God:

I'm told,
"Sometimes it's enough to pray,
'Thank you for the gift of life, today.'
Amen."

And amen.

And amen.

"Good Teacher..." (Luke 18:18-30)
Friday

Rabbi Jesus,

You said it is very difficult for the rich to become
citizens of God's commonwealth.

So, why do I get so nervous
about your call to voluntary poverty,
hoping it doesn't apply to me?

Do the impossible, Good Teacher,
and save us—
we who are rich beyond any reasonable standard—
from our love of wealth,
and from hearts (our own)
too quick to jump to "not enough."

If all we have belongs to you,
tell us when and how to gift it (all)
to the destitute and oppressed.

We ask this in your Name.
Amen.

Emergency Room Prayer (Revelation 22:1-5)
Saturday

God who brings shalom,
Love's own comprehensive well-being:

Bless, we pray, the work of ER personnel.
Sustain them in body, soul, mind, and spirit.
Bring them joy and satisfaction in their work.
Defend them on every side with your peace.

Bless, we pray, their patients:
Some have exercised tremendous courage,
and some, by their choices or circumstances,
must face real or potential disaster.

Through the skill of healing agents,
with the prayers of your friends,
give all of us a taste
of your eternal and transforming life
this very day.

Bring us all, finally, to the New Creation,
where your shalom is the order of things.

In the Name of Jesus, our healer:
Amen.

Lent Five

A Prayer for Our Inner Artists (Galatians 5:22-26)
Sunday

God who teaches us to forgive:

You have made all people in your image,
and channels of your creativity.
But when people mock or stymie that goodness,
their voices stay with us a long time.

Parents tell us, "Get your head out of the clouds!"
Teachers say, "You're obviously not cut out for..."
Even friends cajole us,
"You'll never do it; be reasonable!"

When we hear voices that tempt us toward hopelessness,
give us courage to confront and forgive them,
trusting in your power to release and heal us.

As we forgive, cause us even to bless those who hurt us,
so that our hearts may be clear channels of love;
we even dare to ask, Creator, that you would make us
explosively fruitful—

Make your Spirit's fruit to flourish in our lives.

In Jesus' Name:
Amen.

Meeting Place (Hebrews 10:19-25)
Monday

Trustworthy God:

Sometimes it feels like chaos swallows the world.
Sometimes it feels like fighting is everywhere,
And no one is listening.
Sometimes I find myself thinking ill of my neighbours,
Wondering if they harm me in ignorance alone,
Or whether apathy plays a part.
Sometimes it is hard to remember that you have sprinkled me clean,
Delivering me from an evil conscience.

Sometimes I wonder if meeting with your people is worth it.
Sometimes I am prevented from going—not just for a day, but a long season.
Sometimes I am tempted to despair;
I see so much hypocrisy, strife, harm
done in your beautiful name.
Sometimes, I think I can do better—
so I'd better do it myself.

But…
I find myself hungry for conversation with fellow pilgrims.
I find myself thirsty for loving embraces
from members of the household.
I find myself missing the blessing of peace,
singing together, hearing the Word.

And perhaps most of all, I miss the Table:
Bread and Wine,
Body and Blood,
Manna of Heaven, Medicine of Immortality.
The Meeting Place where I
Behold what we are,
And become what we receive.

Bring me back to that Meeting Place
(and let it be soon):
Even in Jesus Christ, my Lord.

Amen.

On My Side? (Psalm 20)
Tuesday

So, "O King":

What happens when incompetent governments
oppress their people?
What happens when the chariots and horses
trample the poor?
What happens when the Temple doesn't answer?
Or when there is no help from Zion?

What happens when governments
cave to the mob?
What happens when police and military
turn their weapons against BIPOC protestors?
What happens when religious leaders
steal our money?
Or when they
abuse vulnerable people from their pulpits and
the privacy of their 'counselling' offices?

Reading as I usually do,
I read as one of the ones you keep strong,

Someone with whom you are onside—
yes, definitely on my side!

But what happens if I am the one with privilege,
The one with ability,
The one with weaponized 'spiritual' words and tools?

What happens when I forget:
I used to be David,
The runt of the litter,
The youngest who cared for the sheep,
The bearer of food to his brothers,
The one who refused Saul's armor,
The boy who felled a giant with a slingshot?

What if I'm the one praying this Psalm,
Hoping against hope that King Saul won't be
The nasty piece of (wounded) work
He turned out to be?

What happens then?
What does your saving help look like then?

I'm not saying there's no good answer, but…

Sometimes I wish you were predictable,
Like a vending machine,
Coins in slot to buy your protection and
your assaults against my enemies.

Lord, have mercy.

I Wish [Explicit Language] (Luke 18:31-34)
Wednesday

Lord Jesus,

Sometimes, I wish you could be someone
From the Saturday morning cartoons:

Nearly invulnerable, kicking some ass,
Not taking any bullshit, nor even any sass.

Couldn't you have saved the universe without
Dying-on-Cross?

Couldn't I just light a Signal, point it at the clouds,
and *behold!* you'd swoop in to save the day?

I wish you would confer upon me Invulnerability.
Not healing and rescue,
Not liberation and forgiveness.

Yeah yeah yeah,
I know you're trying to tell me about Resurrection.

But seriously:
What the hell are you talking about?

Help Us to be Wise (Hebrews 2:1-9)
Thursday

Glorified One,
Most Beautiful Lover,

This is your answer to the world's evil:
You suffered it yourself, to end it.

O happy day!

Yet we do not see your triumph yet,
and—though if I'm honest my heart thrills
because I trust you—
sometimes it feels like cheating
when I tell this Story.

I want to sing to everyone I meet:
"God has remembered
everything you suffer:
none of it is a waste and
all of it will be put right—!"

But then I sit with someone

who lost their best friend to suicide,
or their parent in a car accident,
or their new spouse to cancer.

I am with them in their hopelessness,
a bright ember burning in my heart.

But telling them of Resurrection,
of the Final Day when you wipe away tears,
is somehow *not* the fitting thing.

Help me—alongside your friends
who want to confront the world squarely
and unclouded—to grow wise
in living the Glad Tidings,
including how, when, and why to say all the things.

In the beauty of hope I pray,
Amen.

When I Grow Up (Hebrews 2:10-18)
Friday

Jesus,

Sometimes when I read of you as the Great High Priest
Or the Cosmic Christ,
I struggle to remember you as a vulnerable baby,
As a struggling carpenter,
As a wandering, tired, prayerful healer,
As someone who laughed without mocking at parties
where everyone was already drunk,
As a male slave willing to wash his own apprentice's
feet—like a Gentile woman.

I struggle to remember
that you suffered when the Devil tempted you,
And yet three little words made him fall silent.

Some of my friends say, about you:
"If he wasn't a sinner like me,
then he wasn't fully human."
They say:
"To err is human—to forgive, divine."

But I can't help but think
There is a crossed wire somewhere,
Some failure of imagination in this thought.

So this is what I want to ask,
While you lift me from my ashes:
Would you gently make me part of your Body,
thus teaching me by degrees to be fully human?

Amen.

Carrying Water (Luke 22:7-13)[4]
Saturday

Jesus,

Let me show your apprentices to the Upper Room,
And let my household's master grant a spacious place
As you prepare to eat the Passover.

Yes, I know I'm carrying water on my head,
An (Essene) man doing a "woman's job" (whatever that means!).[5]
I know it's a gender-queer thing to do in public—
And yet my people will be happy to host you.

Remember me—
and all queer folk who grant you hospitality—
when you come into your Kingdom.

Amen.

---

[4] Inspired by the queer biblical storytelling of Peterson Toscano.
[5] With thanks to Dr David Neelands, Dean Emeritus of Divinity at Trinity College, Toronto, for this historical tidbit.

Passion Week

Shouting (Luke 19:28-40)
Palm Sunday I

Jesus,

When I pray about giving you my voice,
Sometimes I end up giving you barely a whisper:
Shouting about injustice feels too dangerous.

You know, Lord, that I love to shout about you — when I am with your friends.

Give me the courage also to raise my voice,
with candour, clarity, gentleness, and respect,
when "you spread a table for me in the presence of my enemies."

You know, Lord, that I would love to hear the rocks shouting…

But that is not their job.

Amen.

Not What We Expected (Luke 19:28-40)
Palm Sunday II

Triumphant Lord:

Today you came into Zion on a donkey.
Your friends pimped out your ride:
they sensed in their bones that you were the King,
come to liberate the people from oppression.

Their cry—and ours: "Save now!"

But why didn't you cross swords with the Romans, Jesus?
People started to fear.

"This wasn't what we expected of you, Jesus!"

The progressives didn't like you—and we still don't.
Those Pharisees
with their oral tradition
and bodily resurrection
and angels and demons, thus:

"What do you mean, we're abusing the Torah?
What do you mean, a 'non-violent' Kingdom?"

The conservatives didn't like you — and they still don't.
Those Sadducees with their Temple taxes
and Biblical literalism
and political posturing, thus:

"What do you mean, we're fleecing the poor?
What do you mean, we don't need the Temple
anymore?"

And we — pulled back and forth,
harassed like sheep without a shepherd — will cry, only a
few days from now,
agreeing with the agenda of the powers-that-be:

"Crucify Him! Crucify!"

O Triumphant Lord, going to a cross-throne wearing
thorns-as-crown:
You are not what I — what we — expected...

Selah.

YES to You (2 Timothy 1:7)
Monday

O God:

Fear is our enemy, and yours.
"Perfect love drives out fear," reads the Scripture.
In another place, it reads, "God did not give us a spirit of fear..."

O loving God,
that you would expel Fear from my life!
O mighty God,
that you would defend me from it on every side!
O gentle God,
that you would heal and seal
every entryway in my heart and life against it!

In my night, marvelous one, your love embraces me;
therefore, grant me this request, most of all:
That though I must utter a vigilant NO against Fear,
My YES to you would consume my life entirely.

I ask this because of your Radiant Light:

Jesus, the Lord.

Amen.

God's Reputation (2 Timothy 3:10-17)
Tuesday

Faithful God,

About this Book that we Christians claim as yours
(With Genesis at the beginning and Malachi at the end,
Followed by strange things called "gospels,"
An "Acts" that sometimes reads like a travelogue,
Letters by various authors, and an apocalypse dense with symbol
That begs us not to make of it a timetable):

You realise it often makes you look awful, right?
You realise that some of your people are so mean
Because we think you are?

What is "inspiration" supposed to mean
If I am required —
If we are required —
To take everything with equal weight,
Deny science,
Ignore compassion,
Beat up those who disagree with me about

How this library reads
(If not literally, at least rhetorically;
if not with our fists, then by excommunication)?

And yet there arises Someone within the story,
Adam Redux—Love made Flesh,
your own Faithfulness to a covenant
made for a sleeping patriarch—
the One who suffers Violence to exhaust it,
Who snuffs out Death with no lingering smoke.

I trust—I want to trust—this one called Jesus.

What is it like to risk your reputation—
To speak your Incarnate Word—
Before the faces of mud creatures so violent
We can't help but think you are, too?

Selah.

One Flesh (Genesis 32:22-31)
Wednesday

Holy One, Sacred Three:

You call us out of ourselves into communion with each other,
for it is not good that human beings are completely alone.

Yet those who bear the name of Christ
cannot yet agree on what this holy communion
looks like, means, entails.

Can marriage expand to include the same gender?
Is sex before marriage always a sin?
Are faithfulness and monogamy the same?
Must holy queer relationships be marriages?
How do single people fit in?

It is hard to ask these questions because
The voice of the Accuser tells us that to ask means we doubt
the seriousness of your claim on us.

Grant, O God, that we wrestle with all these questions
with wisdom, fresh insight, and courage;
if you must send us away limping,
at least cause us to appreciate the mysteries of our truest
humanity-in-community
with more depth and confident trust in you.

We will not let you go until you bless us!

Amen.

Jesus, Be with My People (Luke 22:39-53)
Maundy Thursday

Jesus, who on this very night
was betrayed by a friend
to suffering and death:

i.
Be with my people,
two spirit-gay-lesbian-bi-trans-queer-plus,
who are betrayed so often by the powers-that-be
(political and religious),
just as you were:

We are often unable to secure dignity and equitable
treatment,
not only before the law,
but in peoples' hearts.

Be with my people.

ii.
Be with my people, disabled-gimpy-crip folks, visible
and invisible,

who are betrayed so often by the powers-that-be
 (political and religious)
just as you were:

We experience systemic injustice,
Oppressions-in-common,
and your Church's lack of healing skill and willingness to lament.

Be with my people.

iii.
But when I am your Judas, Lord:
Forgive me, most of all.

Amen.

Screaming (Luke 23:44-46)
Good Friday

Suffering One:

I know that darkness is a Jewish metaphor:
something huge has changed in the universe.

But people who see solar eclipses, I'm told,
often scream when they happen—
a primal, unasked for acknowledgement of the light,
extinguished.

Is that the moment in which you cried, "My God, my God, why have you forsaken me?"
And were the people screaming with you?

The story says
the curtain in the Temple was ripped in two[6]—
your holiness and the "profanity" of our lives
did not need to be separate any longer.

While we were screaming,

---

[6] Matthew's version adds, "From top to bottom" (27:51).

thinking we were about to die:
you tore up humanity's death warrant,
wrecked the permanent grip of evil,
emptied and annihilated Hell.
Whether or not that darkness was literal,
Thorn-crowned Sovereign,
With all whom you consider friends,
I ponder the word:

"Into your hands I commit my spirit."

Selah.

[...]
Holy Saturday

"Today is the day when God is dead."

Thus writes some wise and reverent poet-theologian,
about this time of waiting between
Cross and Resurrection.[7]

"On this Holy Sabbath, the Creator rested from all his works."

Thus say our Orthodox friends in liturgy.

How much we stand to lose
If this is not the way of things:

Life Himself lies dead in a garden tomb!

O God:
Receive our hearts, full and empty,

---

[7] I think it was Karl Rahner, but I haven't been able to verify this. If any of my readers know for certain, I would appreciate a (dis)confirmation!

As our fitting, though mute, worship.

Amen.

Good Night
Passion Week: Holy Saturday II

Good night,
Best of all Friends:

See you in the Morning.

After the Easter Vigil

O Eternal Strength and Beauty:

Thank you for walking with me, with us,
on this desert journey.
Thank you for common prayer.

Bless those who supported me.
Bless those who prayed with me.
Bless those who struggled, talked, and fought with me.

Continue to shape us into your friends and lovers.
Continue to strengthen us, that we may choose
Life rather than Death.
Continue to pour your love, justice, and shalom
through us to all whom we encounter,
that all might be refreshed.

Remind us always that we are:
people of the Resurrection, heirs of God,
citizens of the New Creation—

and loved beyond all imagining,

the same way you love yourself.

In Jesus' Name:
Amen.

A Triple Alleluia!
The Sunday of the Resurrection of Jesus Christ

All-loving and Sovereign God:

This is the third day, when you raised the Radiant Son,
your good world's Saviour and True Light,
from his rest in a garden tomb. Alleluia!

This is the day when you broke forever
the power of Death, annihilated hell,
and condemned evil in all its forms
to final nonexistence. Alleluia!

This is the day you began the New Creation,
Restored human sonship by adoption in Christ,
and promised that, at the right time,
you would fill all things as the All-in-All,
to the ages of ages. Alleluia!

Christ is risen!
Truly, he is risen!

Alleluia!

Alleluia!
Alleluia!

RW "Robbie" Walker (he/him) lives in Toronto, Canada with his partner. He is a self-described 'queer gendernaut' somewhere on the autism spectrum who lives with Cerebral Palsy, clinical anxiety, and ADHD; as he says, "Good meds are so helpful!" A PhD candidate and Queer Pentecostal theologian, his ministry may yet lead to ordination. His special interests include theology, sexuality, and Star Trek, which makes sense: all three of them are about connection, conversation, and communion with the Other. You can find him here:

Blog: Medium.com/@rob.daywalker
Twitter: @TheologyWriter
Email: rob.daywalker@gmail.com

 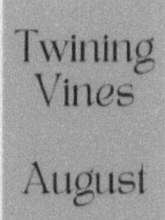 

SQUIRREL HOUSE
2022 LINEUP

titles...

covers...

...and more...

Coming soon!

www.ingramcontent.com/pod-product-compliance
Lightning Source LLC
Chambersburg PA
CBHW030156100526
44592CB00009B/300